This book is property of:

_____

My Picture

Copyright 2022 - All rights reserved.

You may not reproduce, duplicate or send the contents of this book without direct written permission from the author. You cannot hereby despite any circumstance blame the publisher or hold him or her to legal responsibility for any reparation, compensations, or monetary forfeiture owing to the information included herein, either in a direct or an indirect way.

Legal Notice: This book has copyright protection. You can use the book for personal purpose. You should not sell, use, alter, distribute, quote, take excerpts or paraphrase in part or whole the material contained in this book without obtaining the permission of the author first

Disclaimer Notice: You must take note that the information in this document is for casual reading and entertainment purposes only. We have made every attempt to provide accurate, up to date and reliable information. We do not express or imply guarantees of any kind. The persons who read admit that the writer is not occupied in giving legal, financial, medical or other advice. We put this book content by sourcing various places

.Please consult a licensed professional before you try any techniques shown in this book. By going through this document, the book lover comes to an agreement that under no situation is the author accountable for any forfeiture, direct or indirect, which they may incur because of the use of material contained in this document, including, but not limited to, — errors, omissions, or inaccuracies.

Letter Hunt

Find and color the letter A

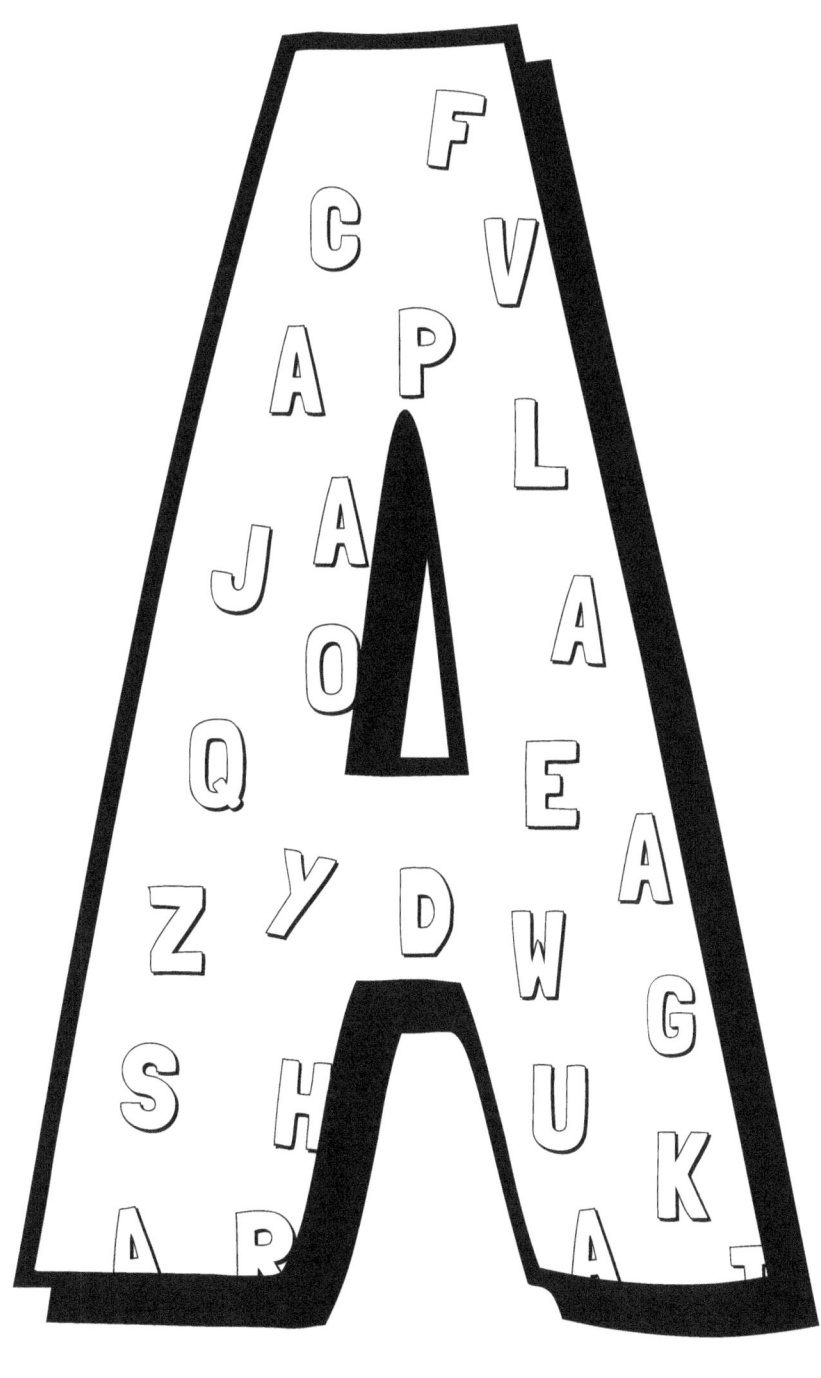

Aa

Letter Hunt

Find and color the letter B

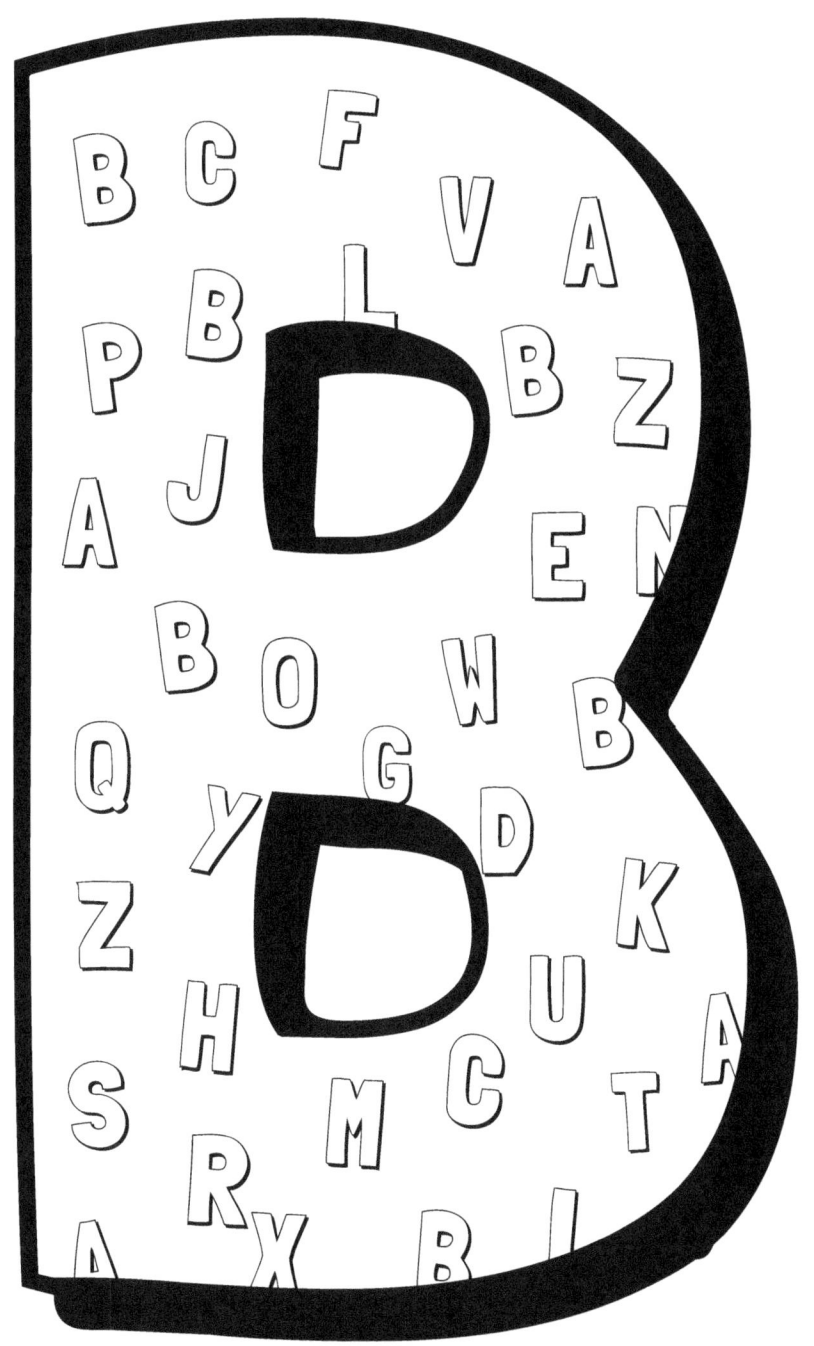

B b

Letter Hunt
Find and color the letter C

Cc …… …… …… …… …… …… …… …… …… …… …… …… ……

Letter Hunt

Find and color the letter D

D d

Letter Hunt

Find and color the letter E

E e ....

Letter Hunt

Find and color the letter F

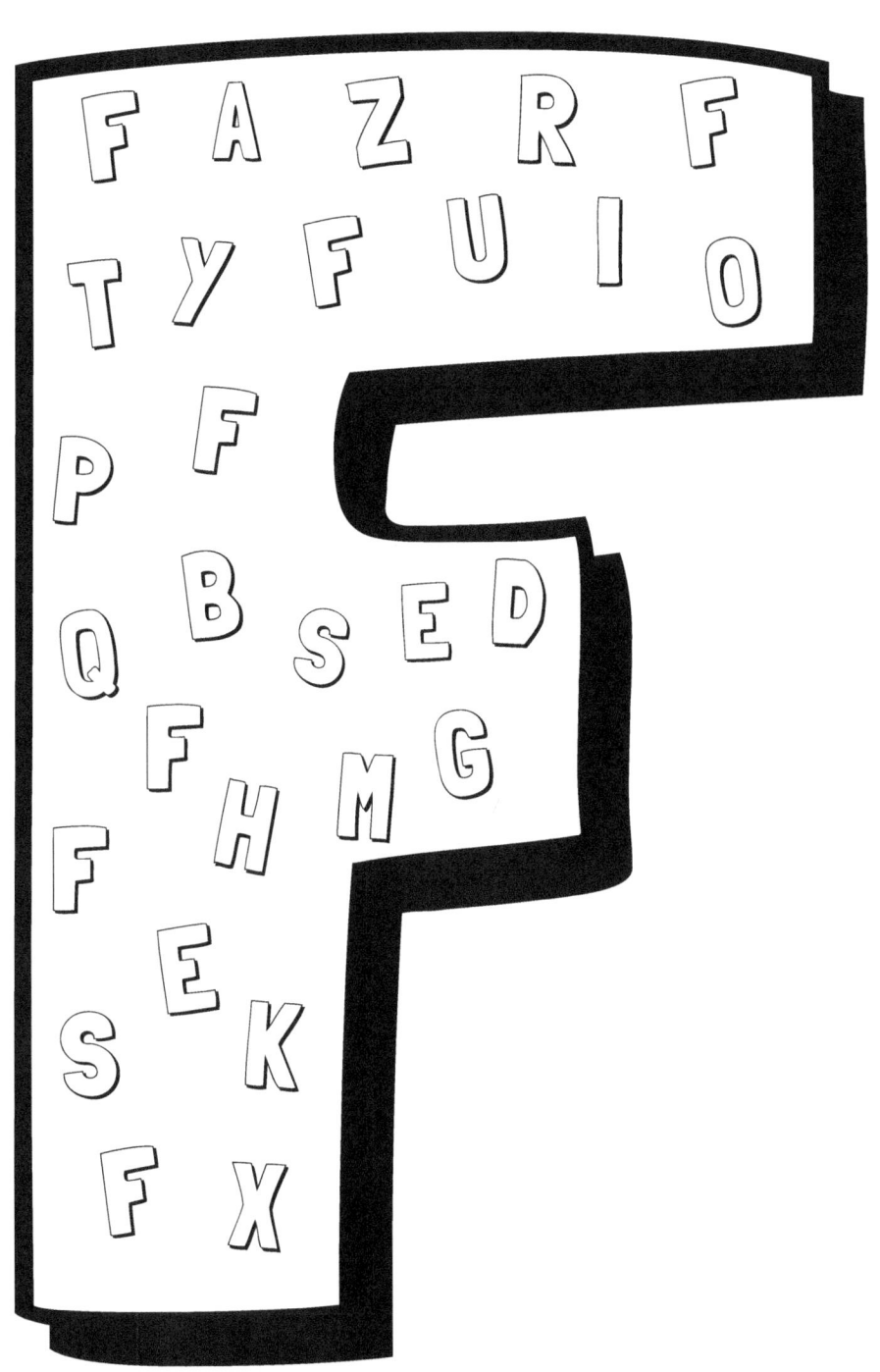

F f

Letter Hunt

Find and color the letter G

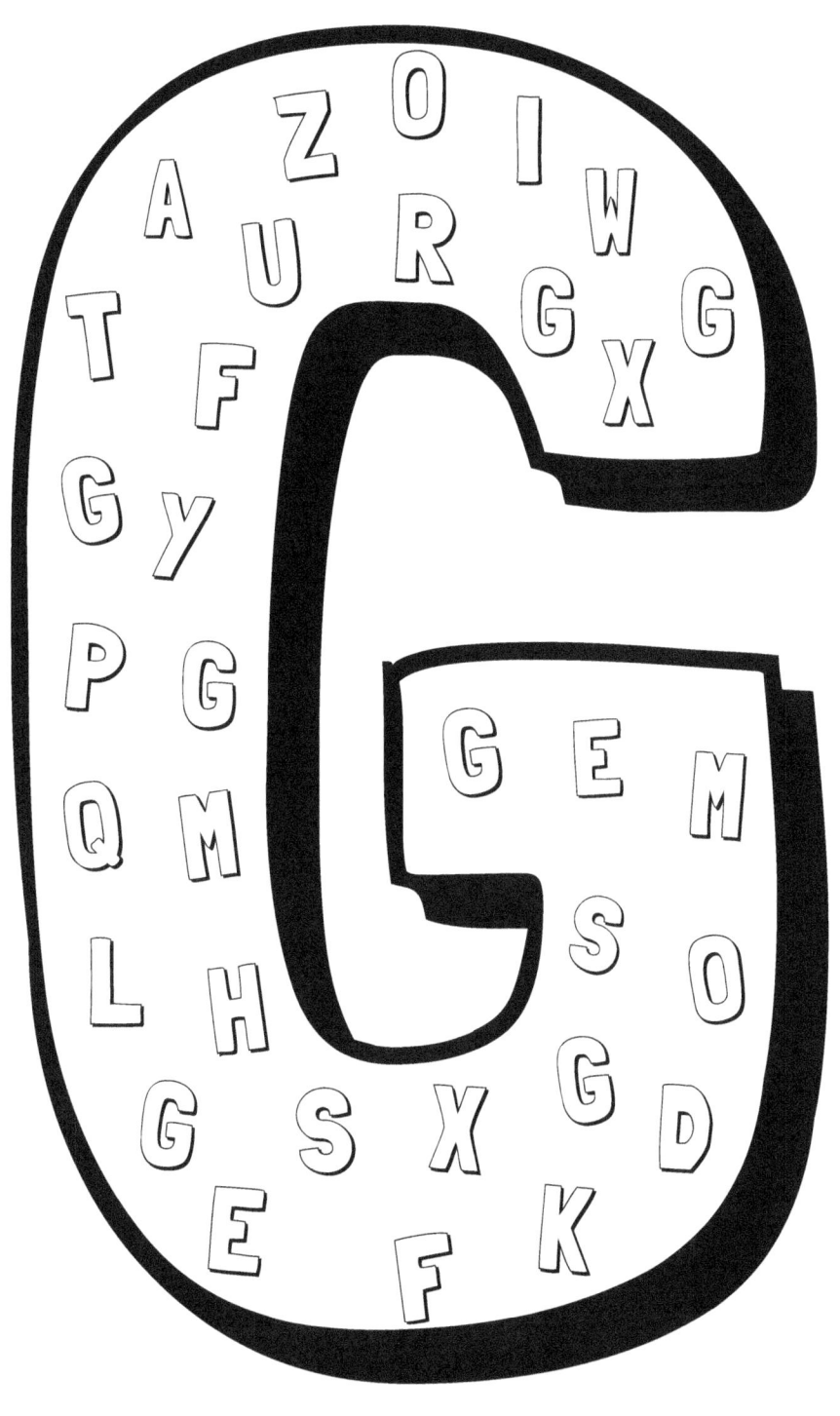

G g

Letter Hunt

Find and color the letter H

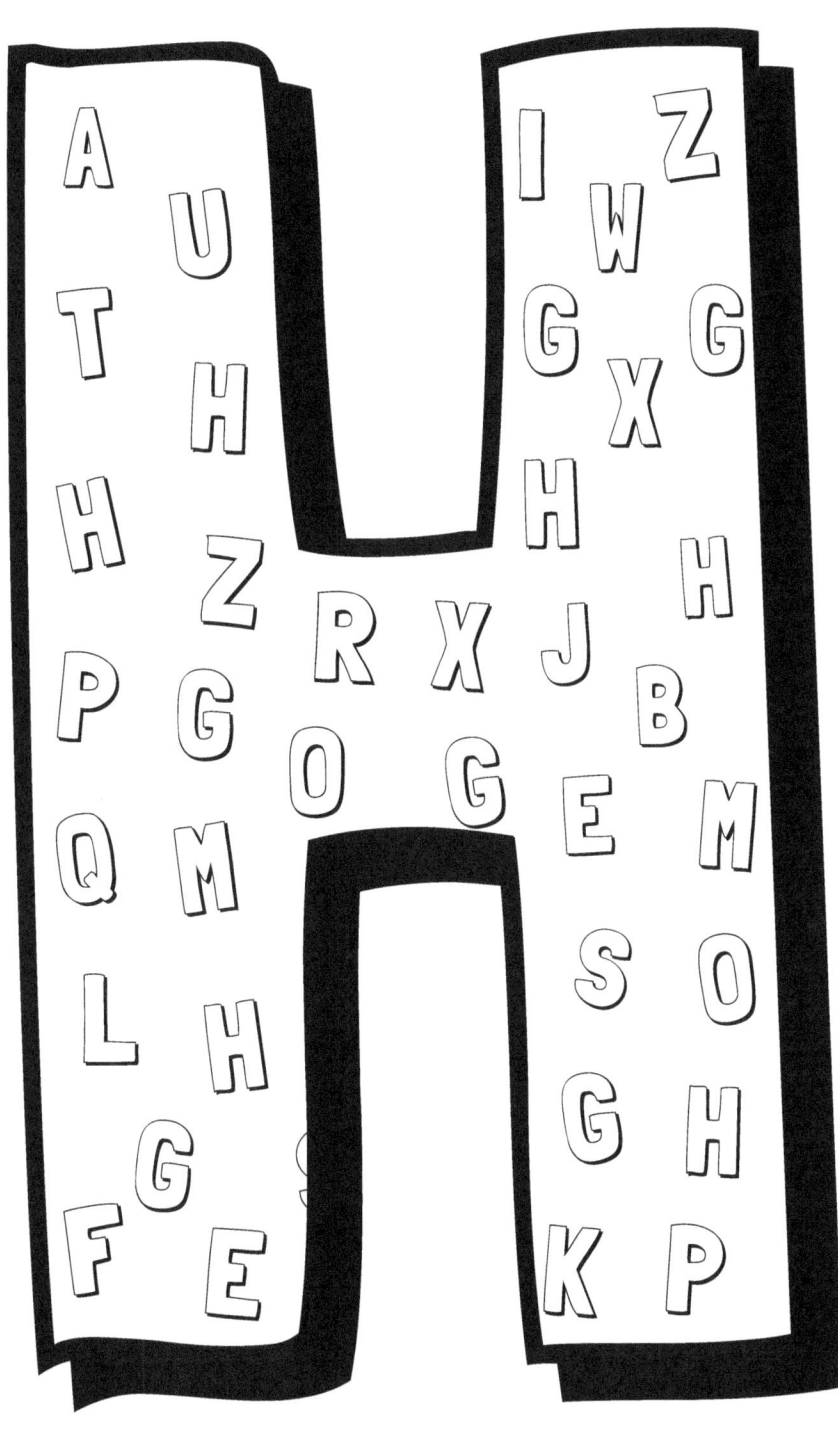

H h

Letter Hunt

Find and color the letter I

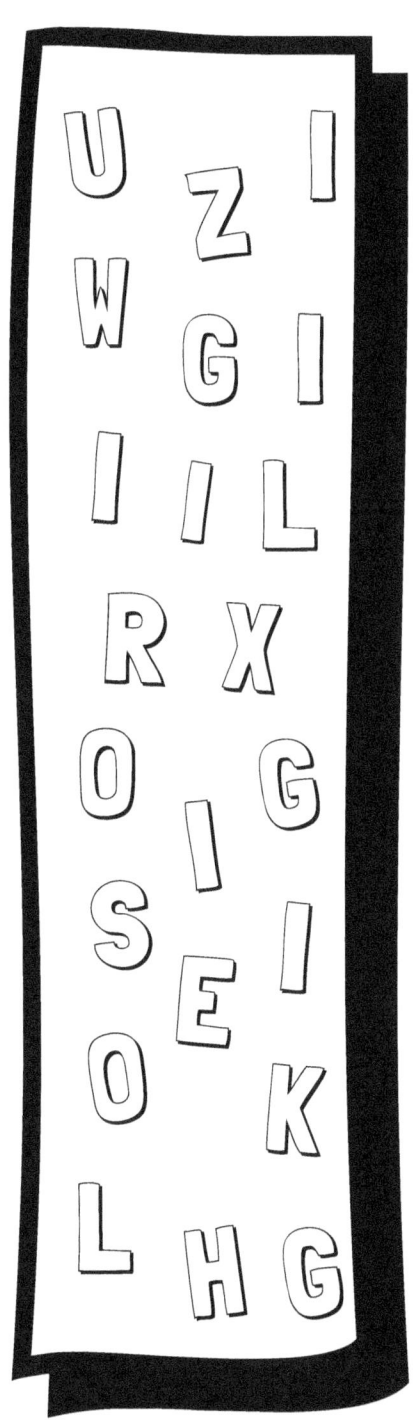

I i ………………………………………………

Letter Hunt

Find and color the letter J

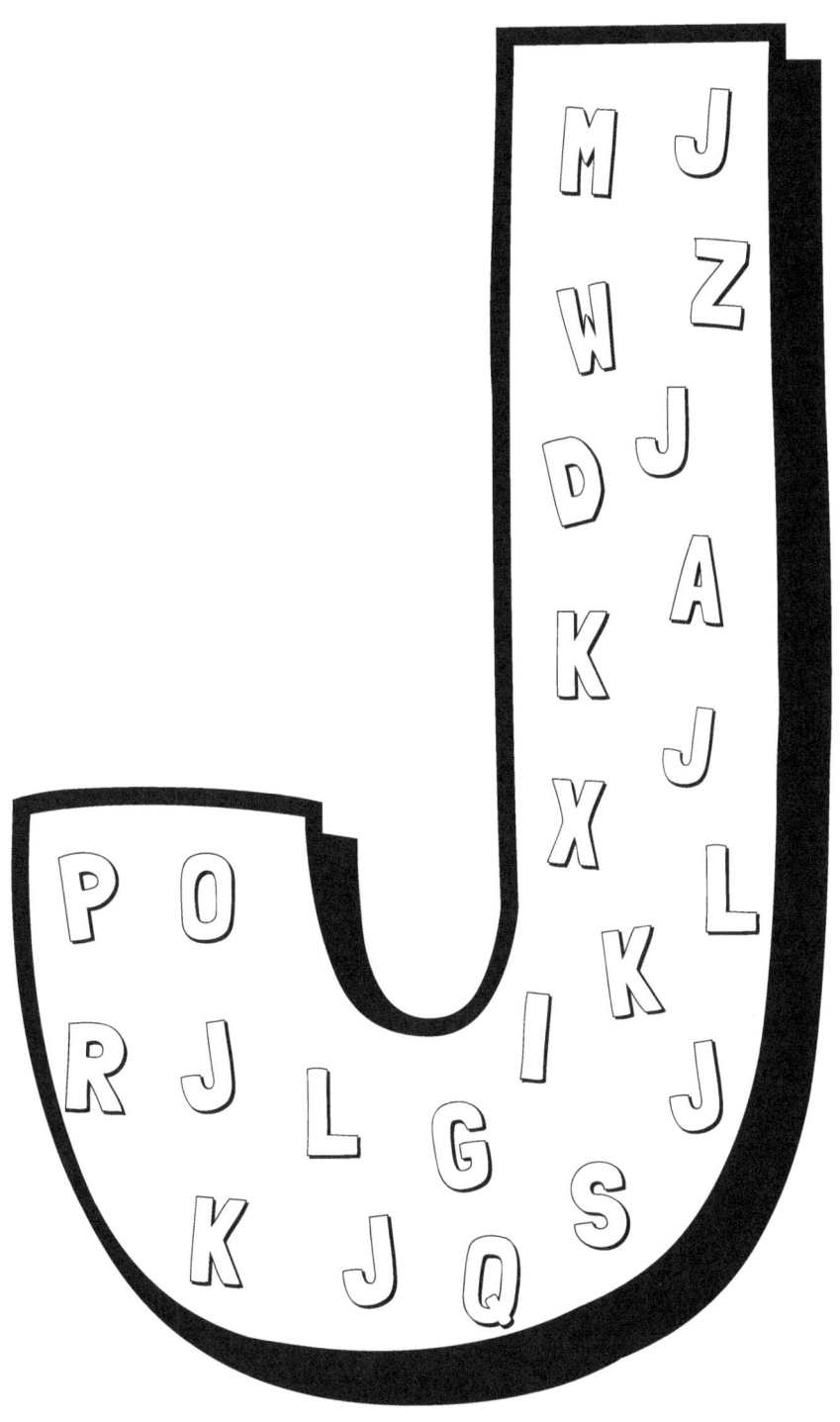

J j

Letter Hunt

Find and color the letter K

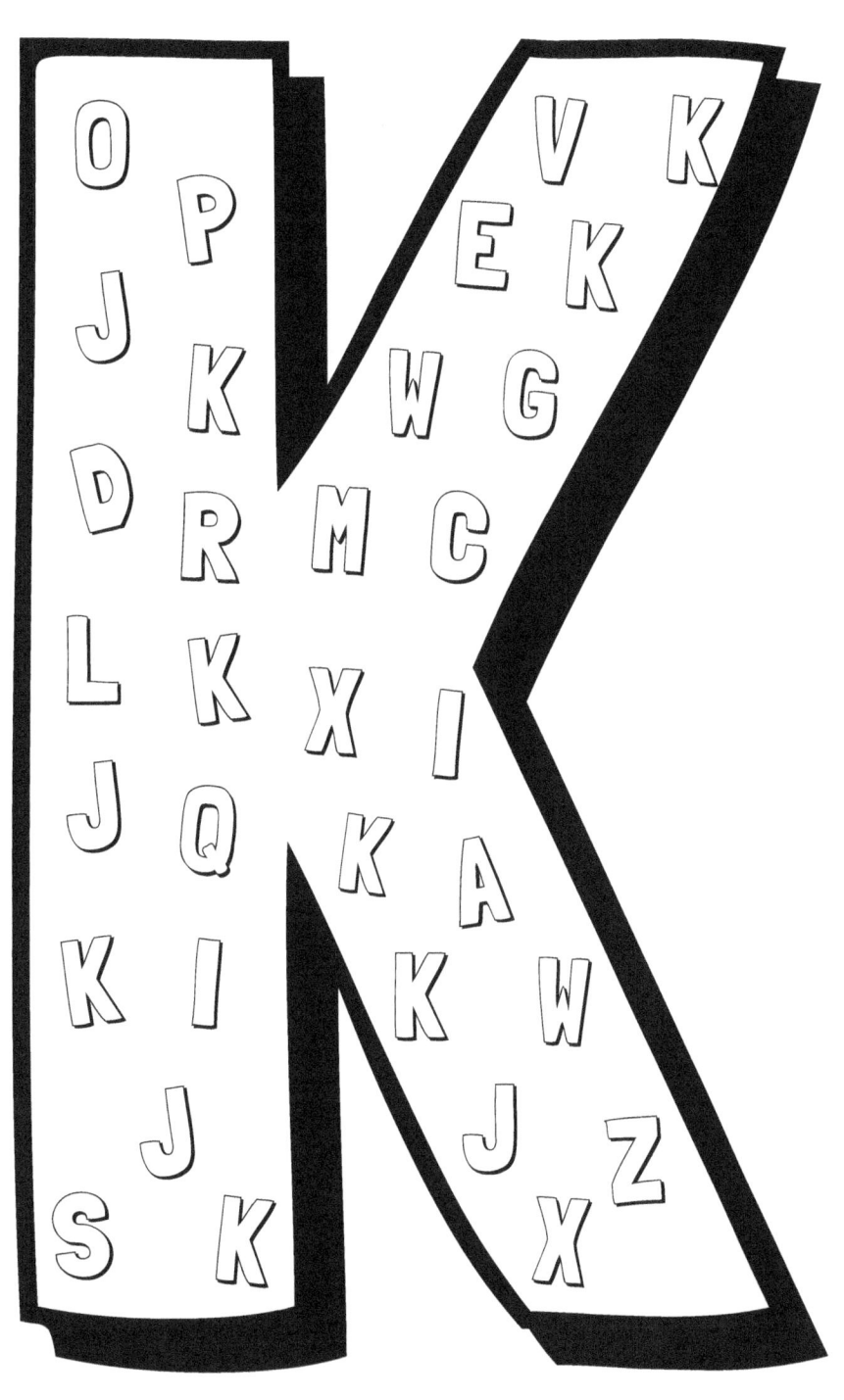

K k

Letter Hunt

Find and color the letter L

L l ………………………………………………………

Letter Hunt

Find and color the letter M

M m

Letter Hunt

Find and color the letter N

N n … … … … … … … … … … … … … … … … …

… … … … … … … … … … … … … … … … … …

… … … … … … … … … … … … … … … … … …

… … … … … … … … … … … … … … … … … …

… … … … … … … … … … … … … … … … … …

… … … … … … … … … … … … … … … … … …

… … … … … … … … … … … … … … … … … …

… … … … … … … … … … … … … … … … … …

… … … … … … … … … … … … … … … … … …

… … … … … … … … … … … … … … … … … …

… … … … … … … … … … … … … … … … … …

… … … … … … … … … … … … … … … … … …

… … … … … … … … … … … … … … … … … …

… … … … … … … … … … … … … … … … … …

… … … … … … … … … … … … … … … … … …

Letter Hunt

Find and color the letter O

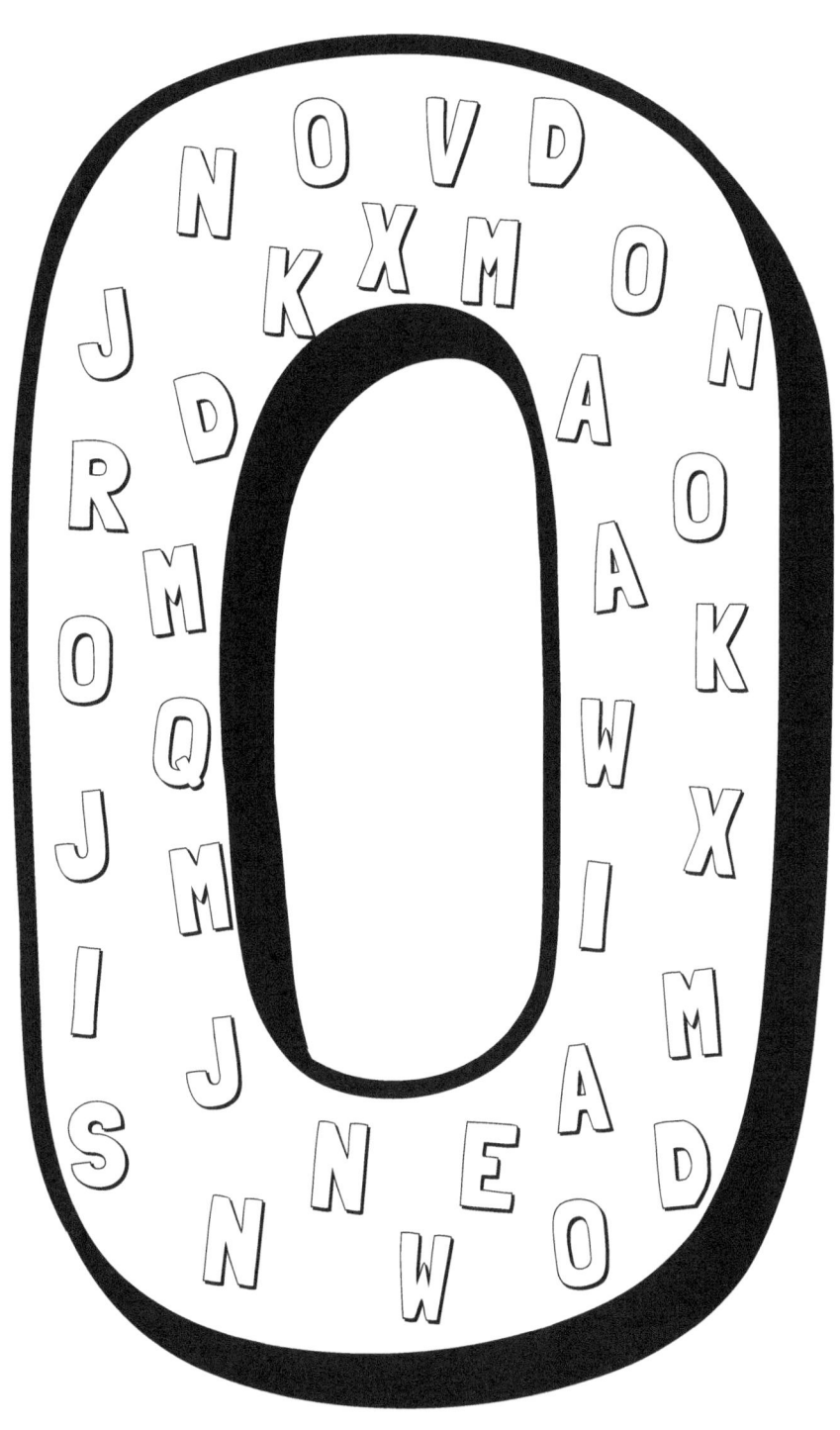

O o

Letter Hunt

Find and color the letter P

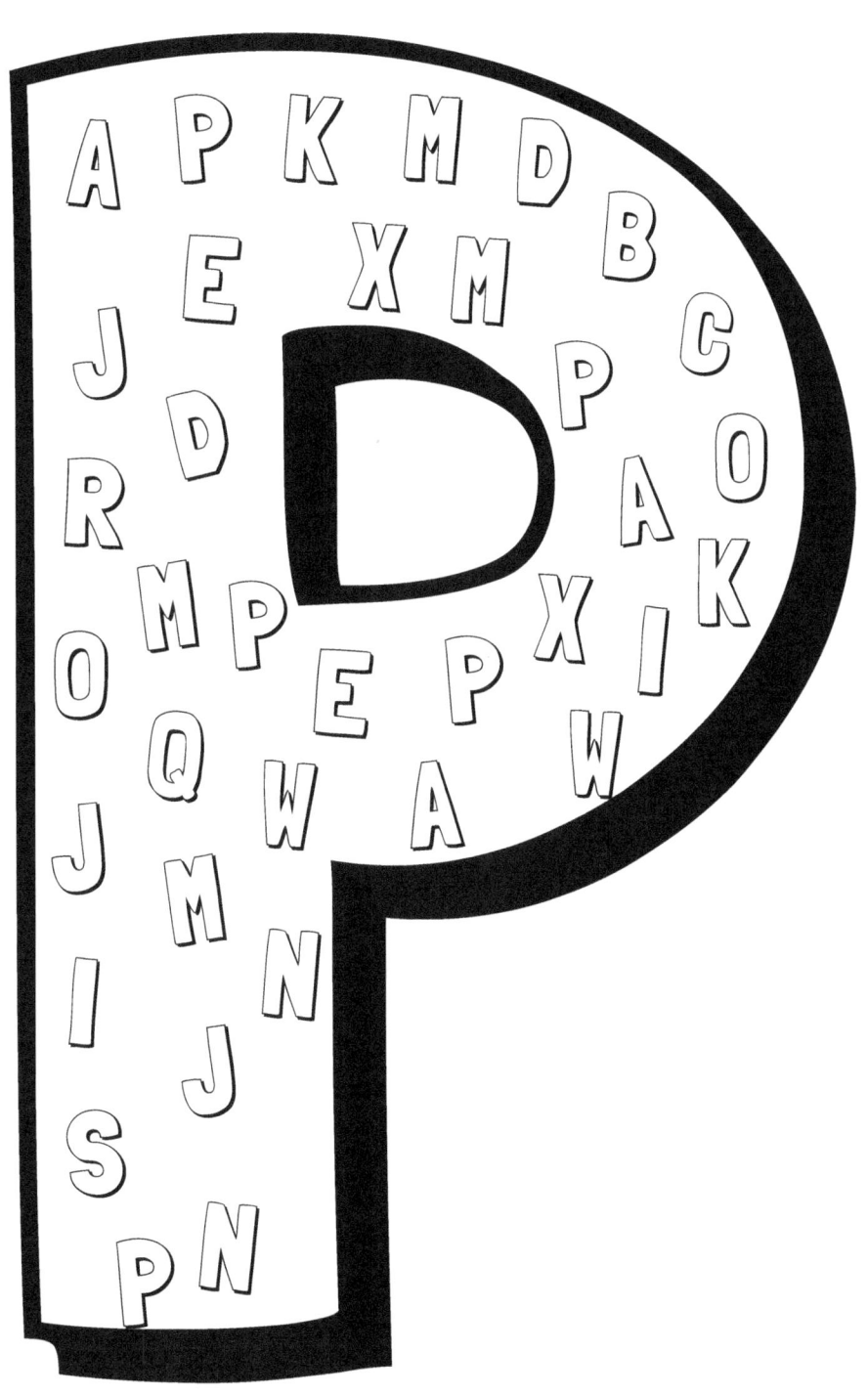

P p

Letter Hunt

Find and color the letter Q

Q q

Letter Hunt

Find and color the letter R

R r

Letter Hunt

Find and color the letter S

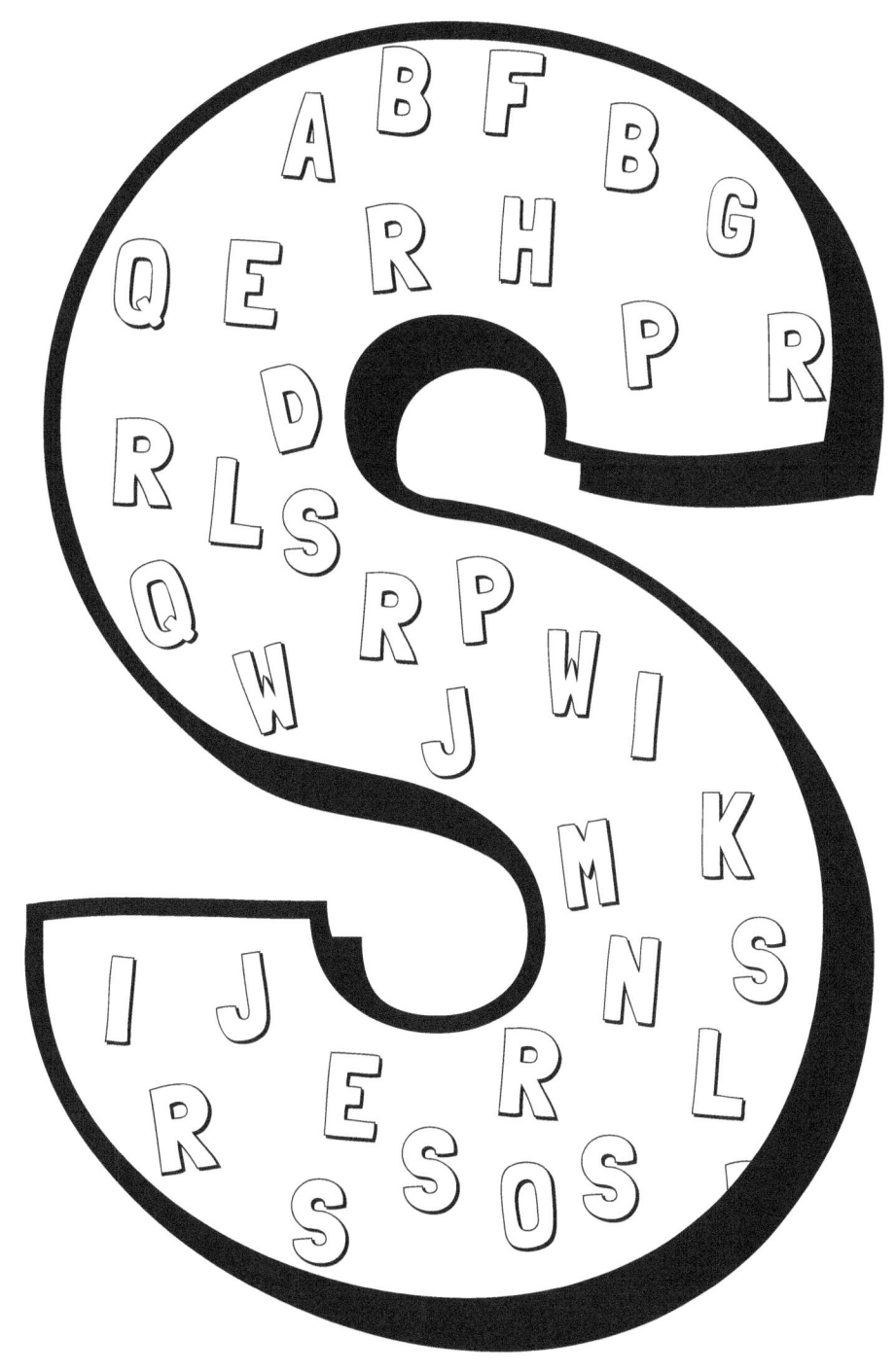

S s

Letter Hunt

Find and color the letter T

Tt ……………………………………………………………………

Letter Hunt

Find and color the letter U

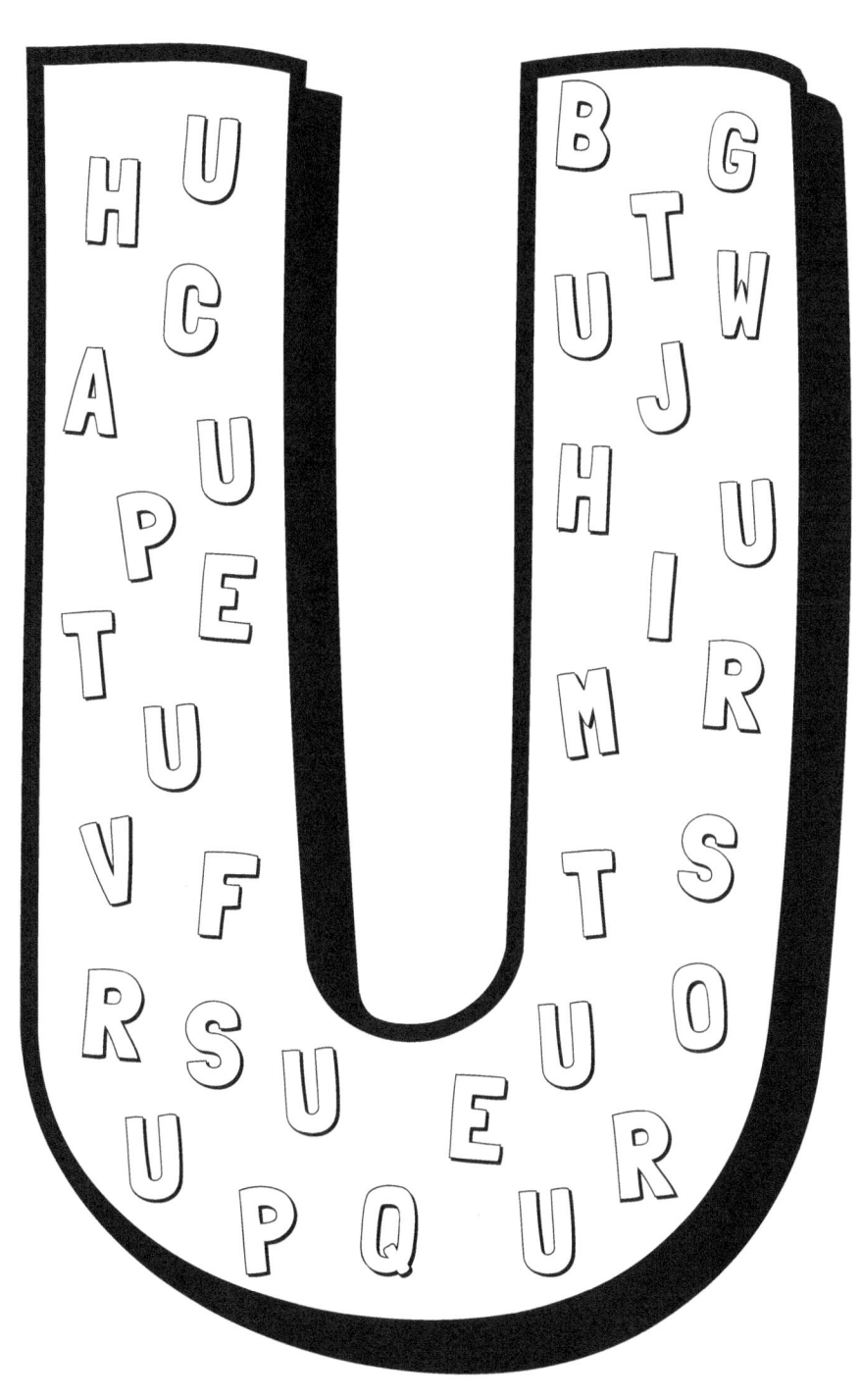

U u ……………………………………………………

………………………………………………………………

………………………………………………………………

………………………………………………………………

………………………………………………………………

………………………………………………………………

………………………………………………………………

………………………………………………………………

………………………………………………………………

………………………………………………………………

………………………………………………………………

………………………………………………………………

………………………………………………………………

………………………………………………………………

………………………………………………………………

Letter Hunt

Find and color the letter V

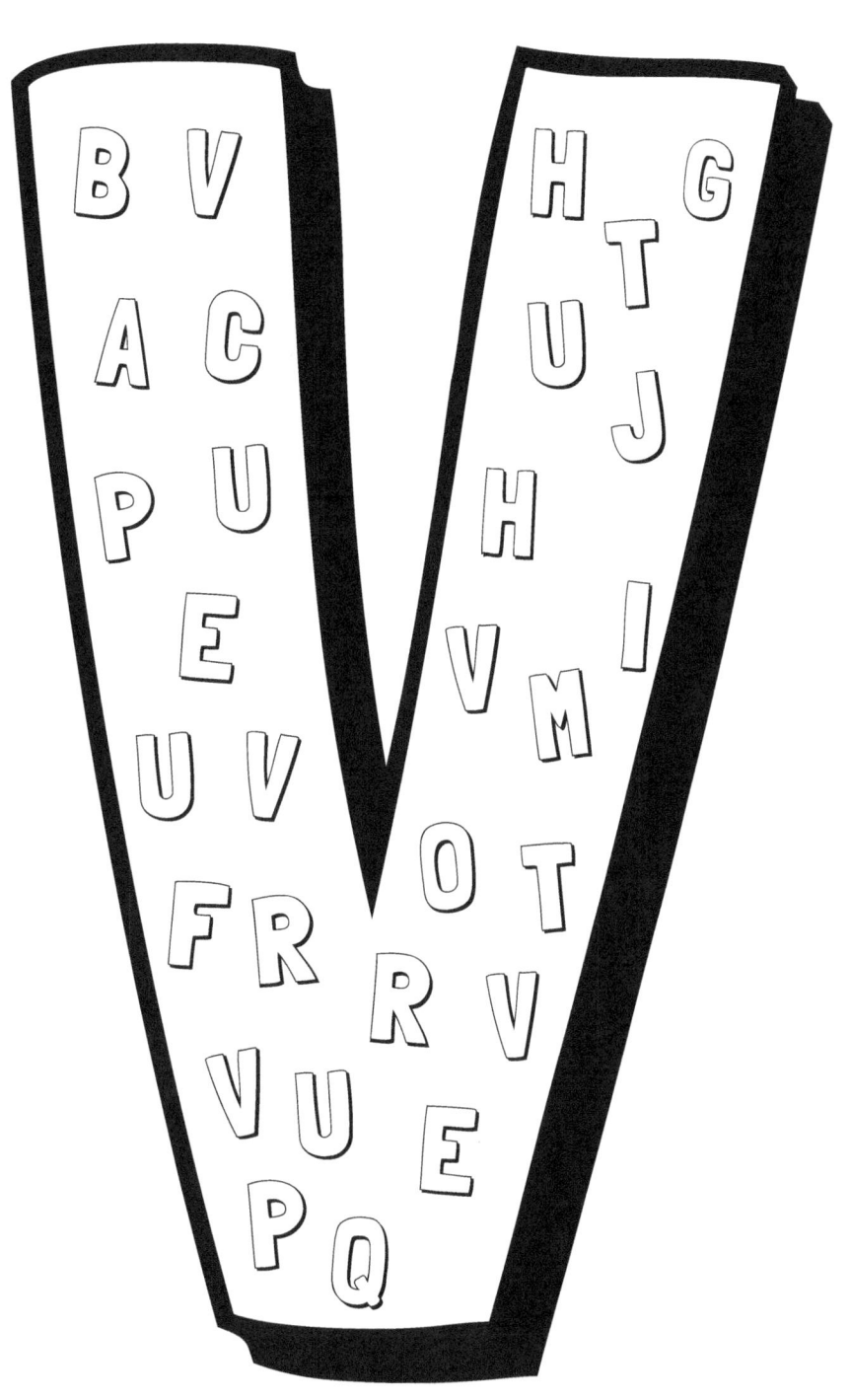

V v

Letter Hunt

Find and color the letter W

W w

Letter Hunt

Find and color the letter X

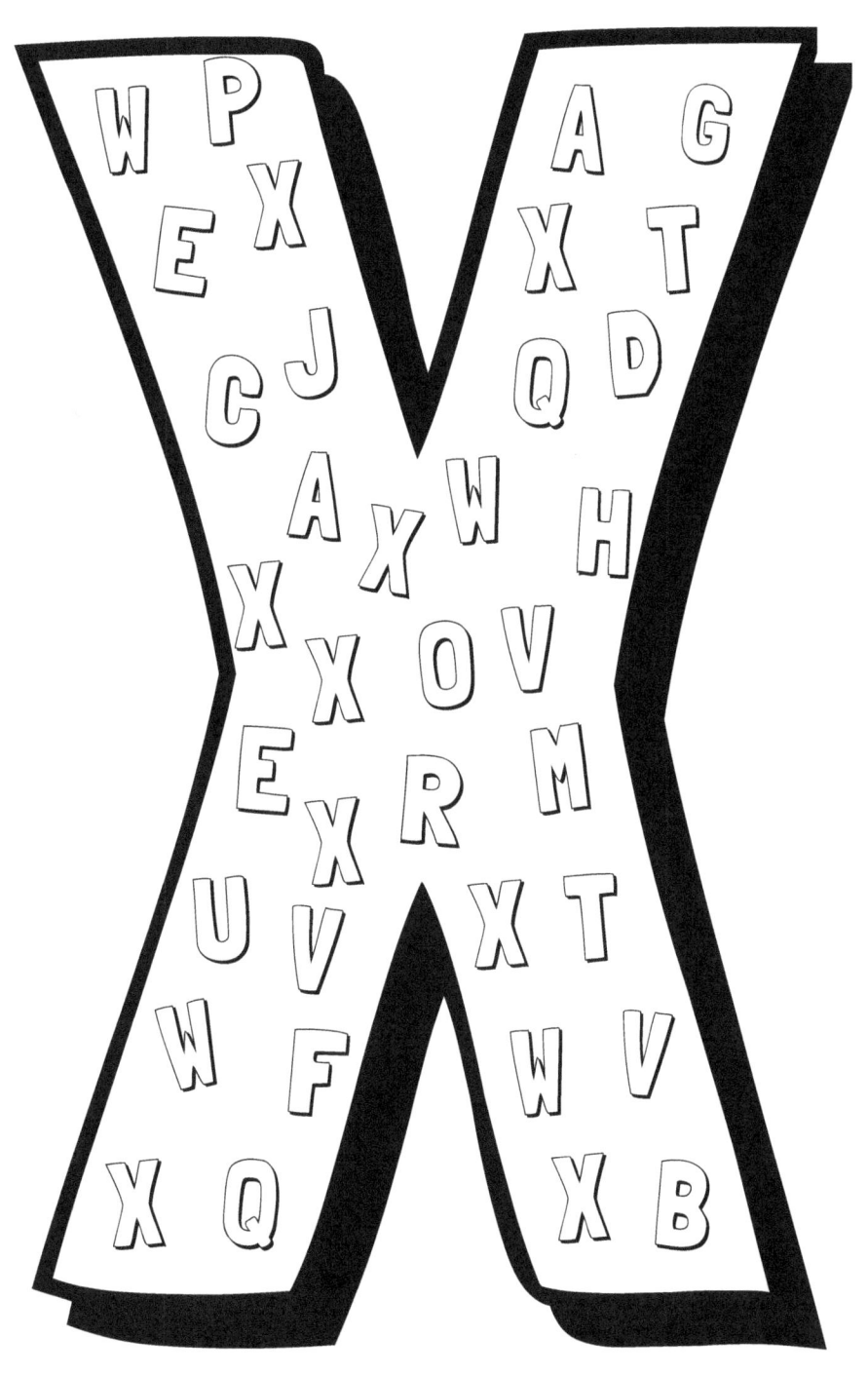

X x

Letter Hunt

Find and color the letter Y

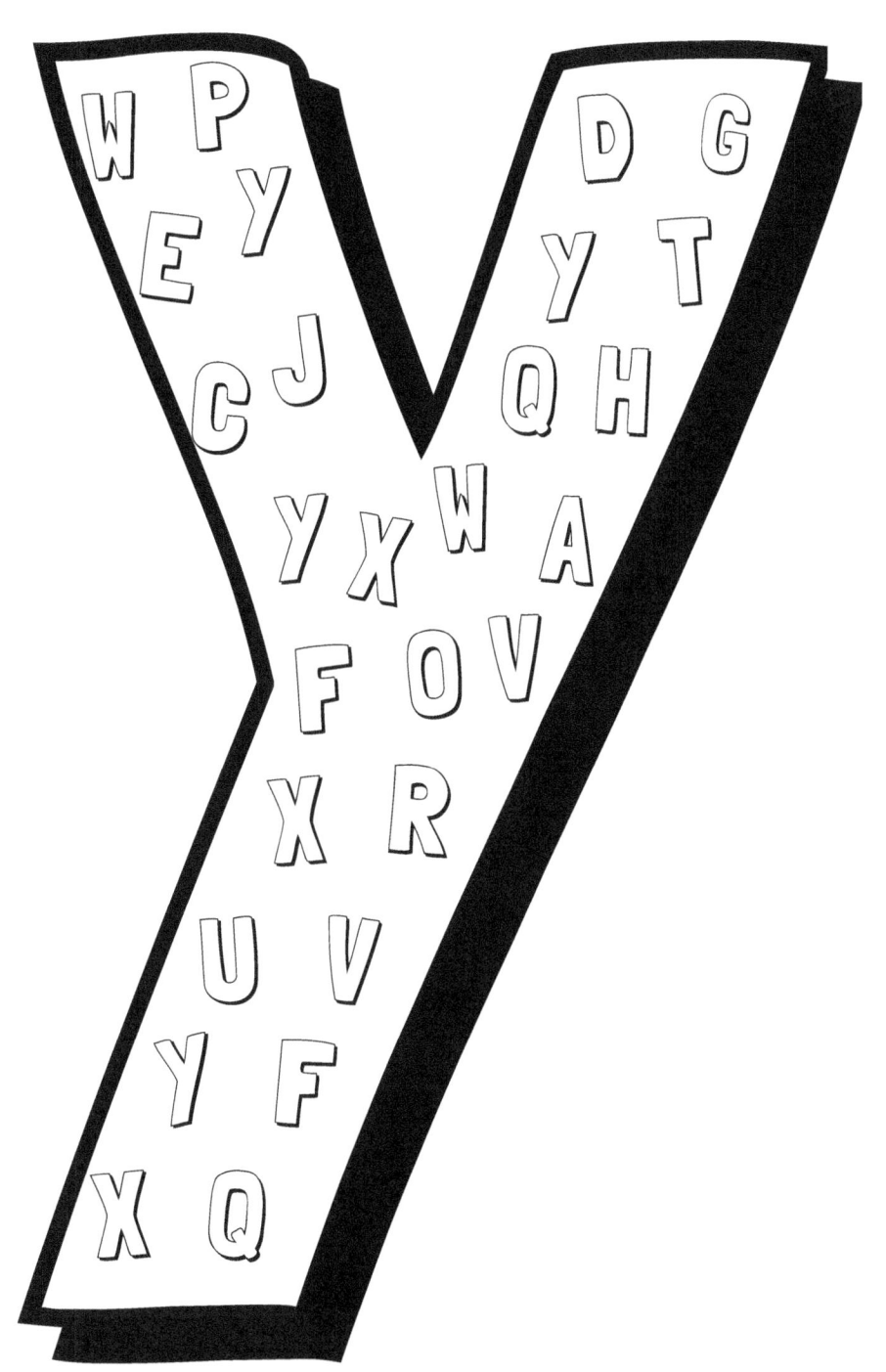

Y y

Letter Hunt

Find and color the letter Z

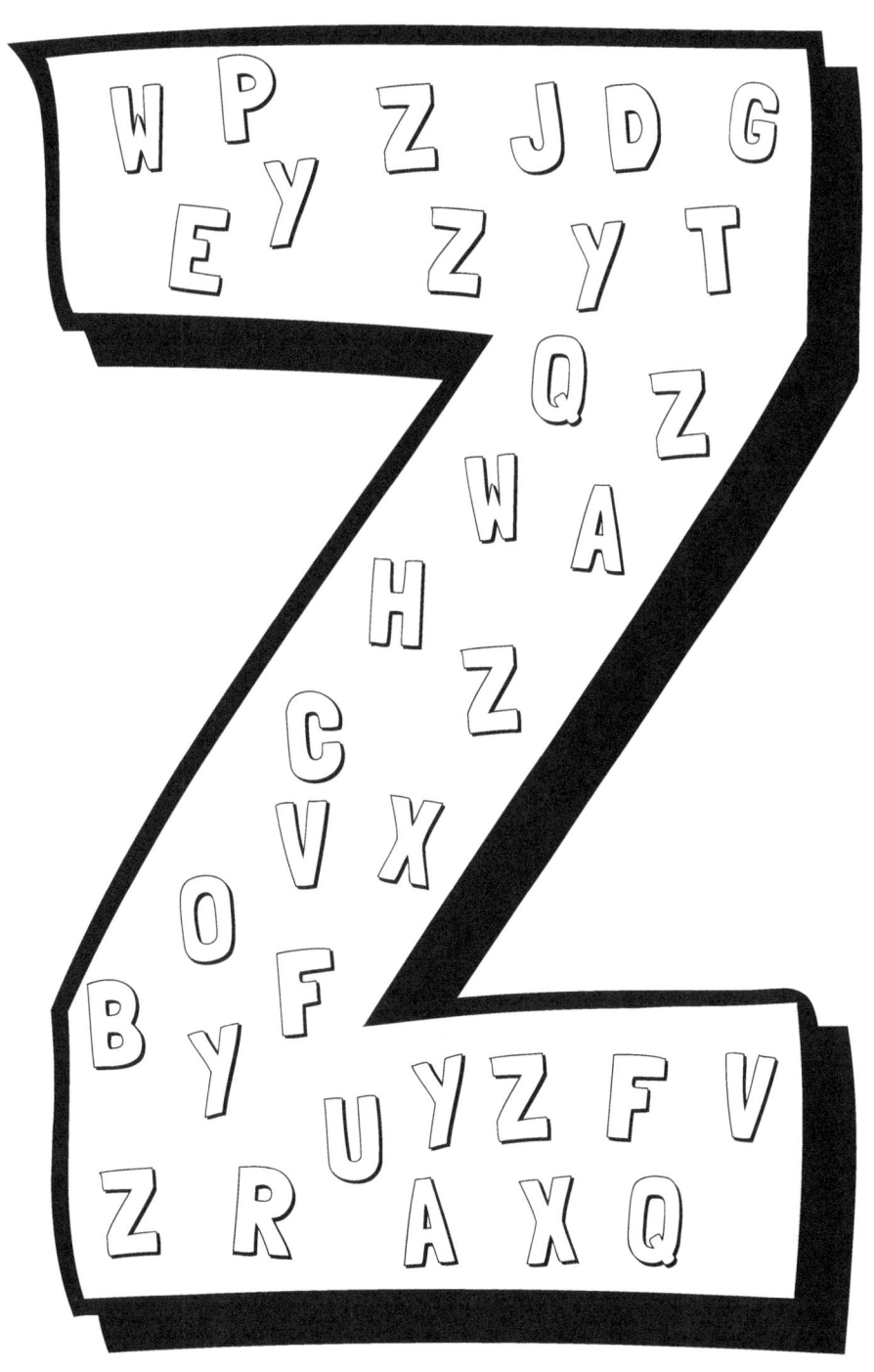

Z z ……………………………………………………………………

Letter Hunt

Find and color the letter Z

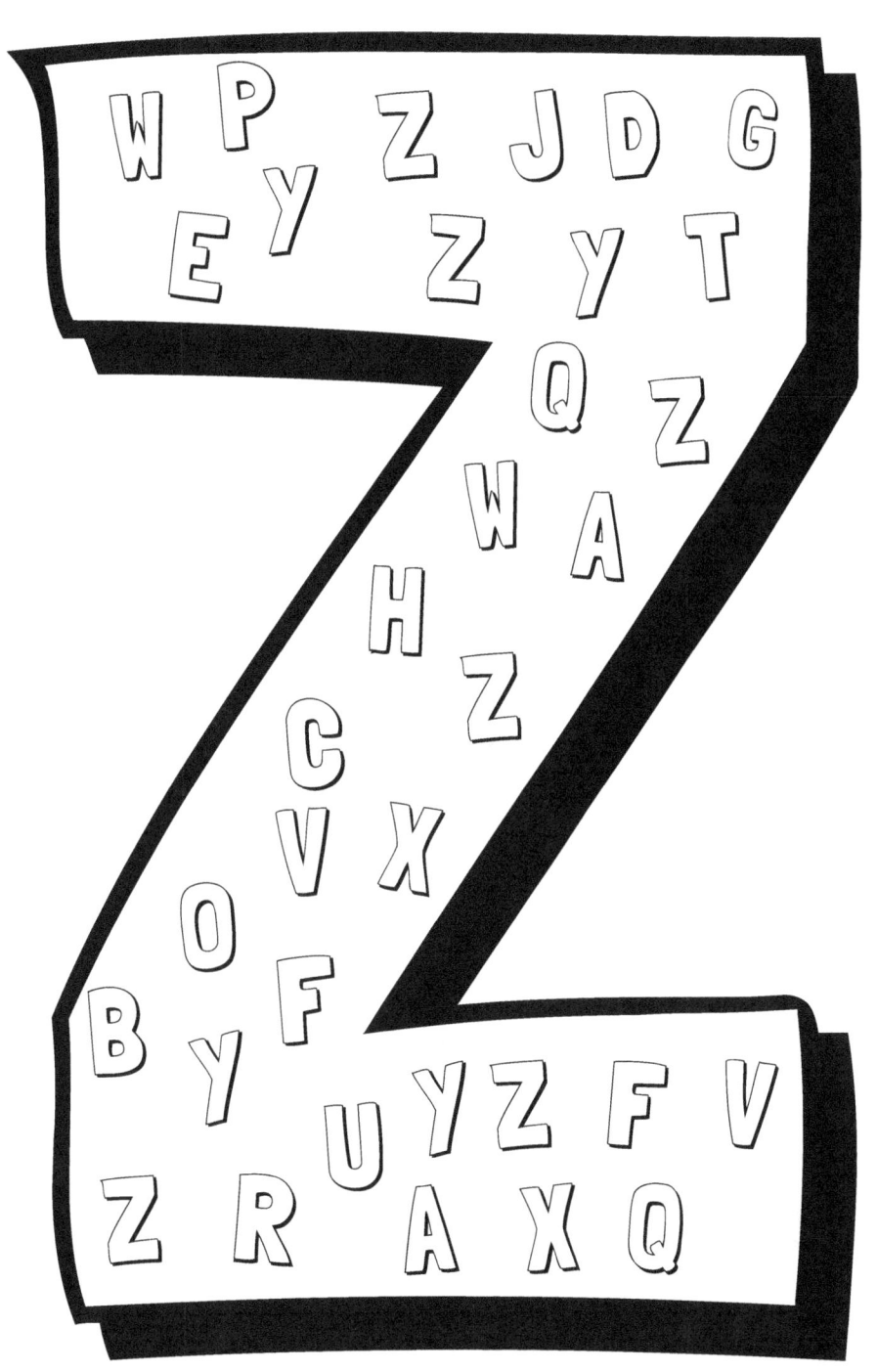

Zz

□   ... ...

... ...

... ...

... ...

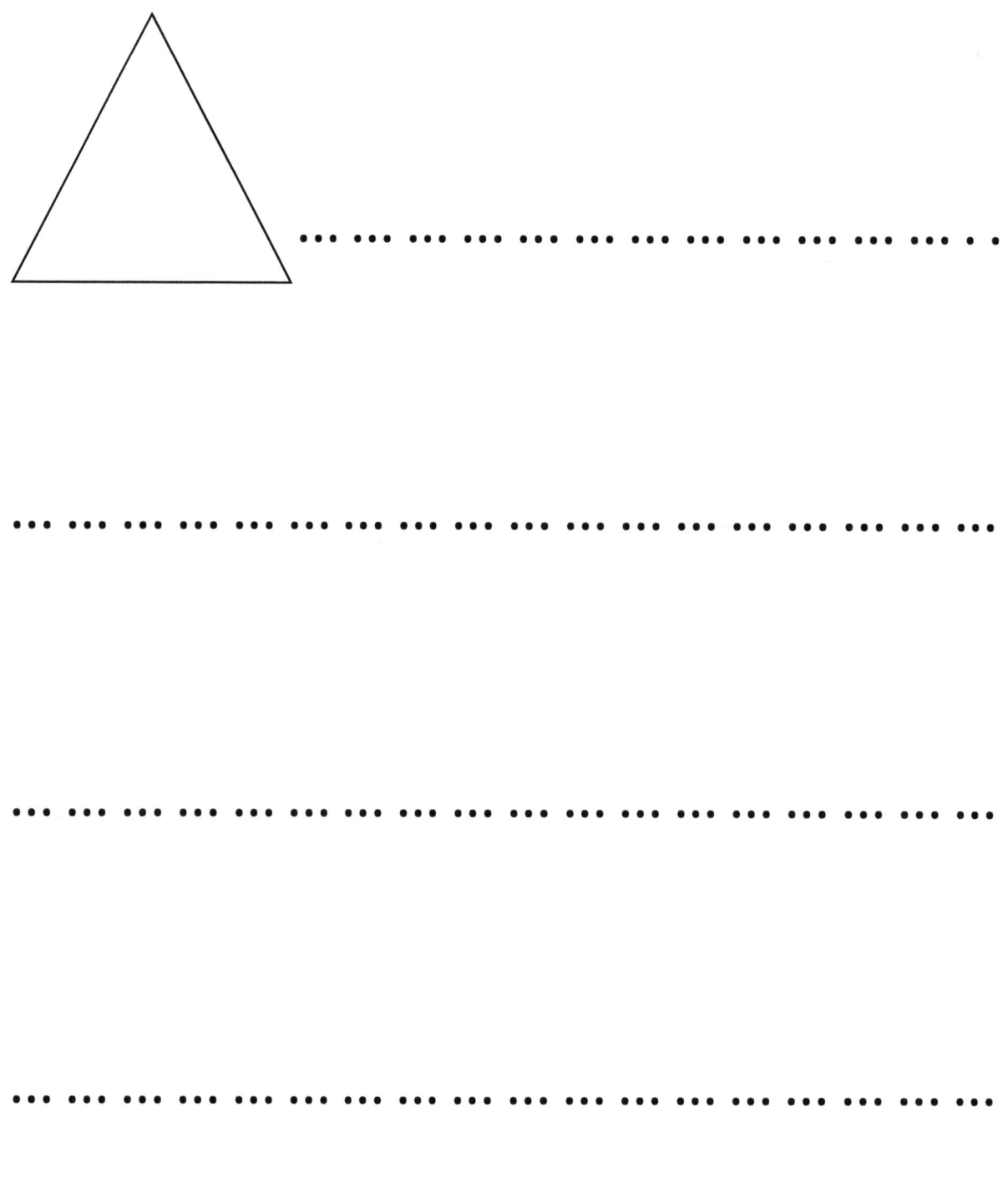

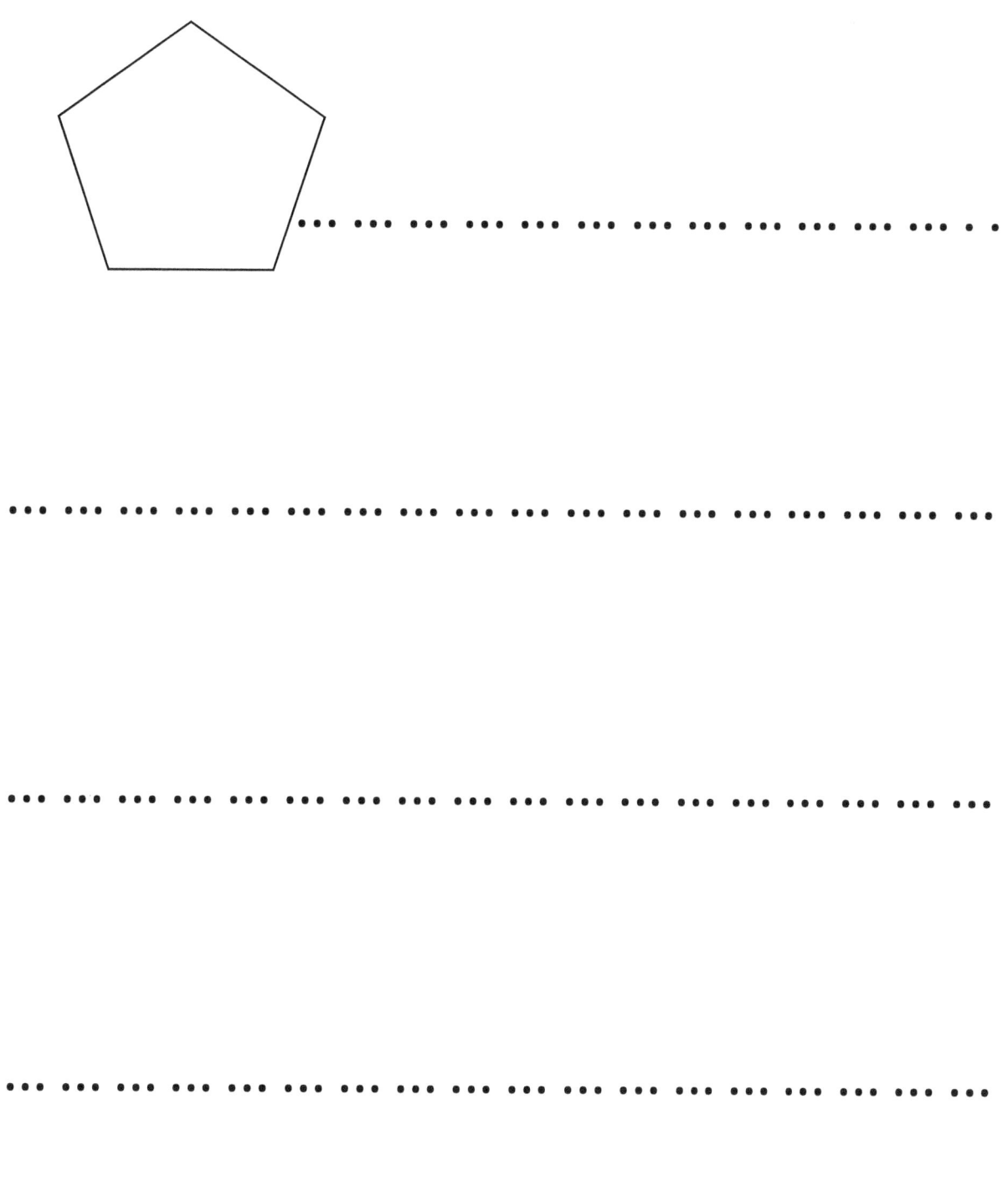

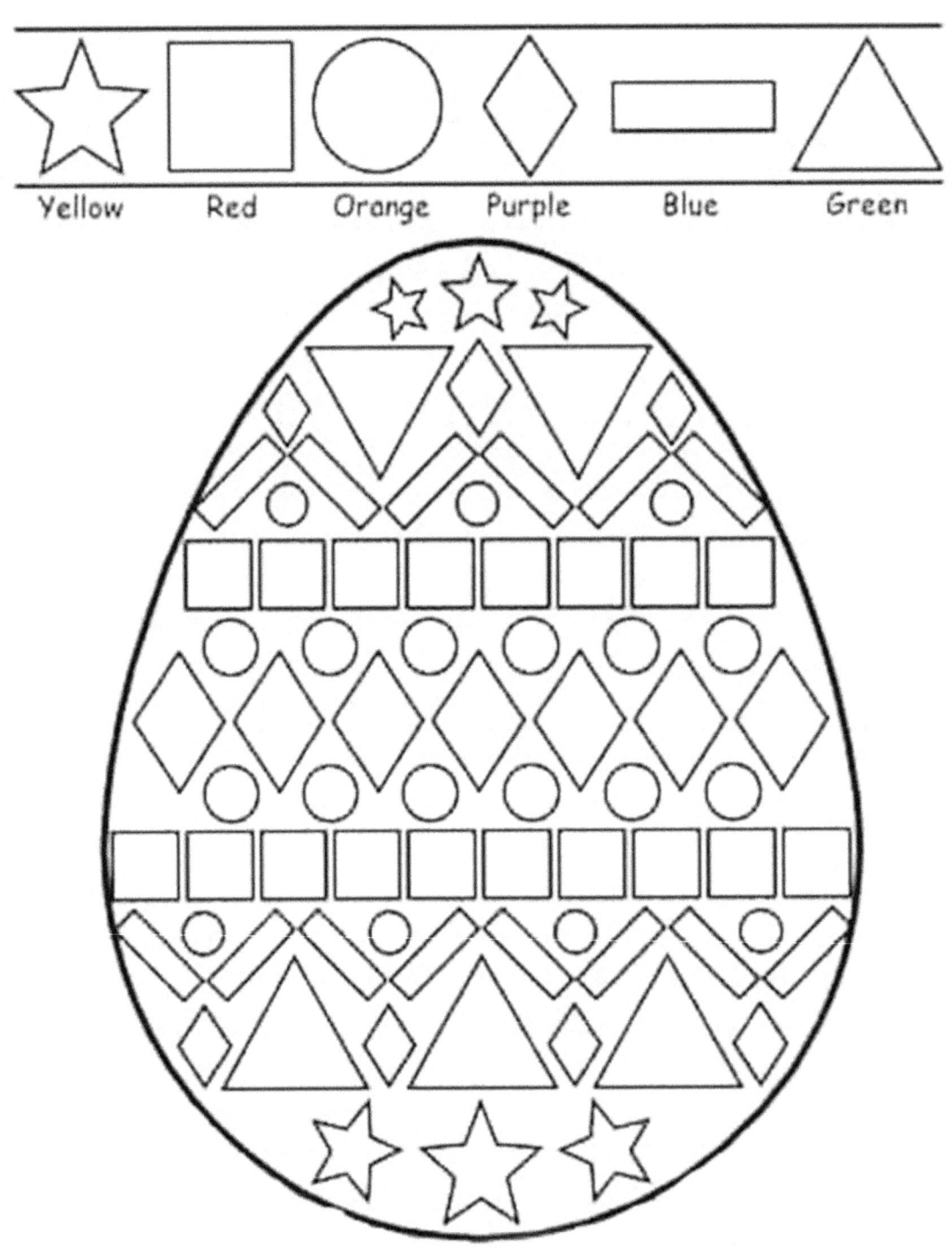

Color the shapes accordingly

Color the Egg!

Color the Egg!

Color the Basket!

Draw your own creation

Can you help mommy find her way to her baby? Do this by marking the dots. You're allowed to use a dot more than once.

FUN FRUIT COLORING

FAST FOOD
COLORING

Thank you.

We hope you enjoyed our book

As a small family company, your feedback is very important to us.

Please let us know how you like our book at:

happypublishing2021@gmail.com

FAST FOOD
COLORING

Thank you.

We hope you enjoyed our book

As a small family company, your feedback is very important to us.

Please let us know how you like our book at:

happypublishing2021@gmail.com